Stings in Tails

Virgilio Goncalves

Stings in Tails

Acknowledgements

Some of the poems in this anthology have appeared, at times in different forms, in the following publications:
One Life: Two Lands, A Migrant's Perspective (1997)
Poetry through a Lens (2013)
Anchored on Eyre (2013)
Voices on the Waves (2013)
Ochre, an anthology (2014)
The Milang Community News (2017)
tamba (2018)

Thanks to my wife, Lesley, always the voice of reason.

Also to Jude Aquilina, who encouraged me to expose my poems to public scrutiny, and for her editing suggestions, many of which I gladly took on board.

Thanks, too, to those who selected 'Attitude' as the winner of the Gawler Poetry Prize in 2016. That thumbs-up gave me the confidence to produce this body of work.

Finally,
Eyre Writers (on the Eyre Peninsula)
University of the Third Age in Aldinga Beach
Ochre Coast Poets group (based in Seaford)
– thank you. You have all played roles in my development as a writer.

Stings in Tails
ISBN 978 1 76041 622 5
Copyright © text Virgilio Goncalves 2018
Cover photo: Scorpion in Thailand and Southeast Asia,
by apisitwilaijit29

First published 2018 by
GINNINDERRA PRESS
PO Box 3461 Port Adelaide 5015 Australia
www.ginninderrapress.com.au

Contents

Part 1 The World Around Us	9
Liaison	11
Real World	12
Desire	13
Fragments	14
Homeless	15
On the Farm	16
Wonder Drug	17
Two Roses	18
Now What?	19
Contrast	20
Living the Dream	21
Mother Worries	22
Who's the Boss Then?	23
Always There	25
Pointless	26
Ostrich Palace	27
Missing You	28
Nightlife	29
Part 2 Shades of Bleak	31
Why Him?	33
Tangled Web	35
Senseless	36
A Mother's Grief	37
On the Precipice	38
Merrilyn	40
The Parting	41
Changing World 1	42
Changing World 2	43

Through My Eyes	44
Caged Within	46
Mind-field	47
Lucky Us	48
Street Cents	49
Dis o r d e r	50
Alfred	51
Apart	52
Lottery	53
Lost Chance	54
Stranger in Silk	55
Stepping Stones	56
Eerie	57
Part 3 Let in the Light	**59**
Attitude	61
Horror Show	63
Dad's Delight	64
Can't Live Without You	65
Face of Change	66
All Together Now	67
Gimme Five	68
Ship Shapes	69
Grandpa's Lament	70
New Breed	72
Carpe Diem	73
Young Mind	74
Seat Lotto	75
Colour Coded	77
Odd One Out	78
Glassy-eyed	79
Spicy Scandal	80
Last Strand	82

Travel Tribulations	83
Too Close for Comfort	84
Fired Up	85
Remember When	86
Part 4 Water Runs Deep	**87**
Locomotion	89
Just a Shoe	91
Casting a Spell	92
As One	93
Satisfaction	94
Watchful Eye	95
After the Drowning	96
Bonding	97
Kicking Back	99
Ice Breaker	100
Quiet	101
Serenity	102

Part 1

The World Around Us

Come forth into the light of things,
let nature be your teacher.

William Wordsworth

Liaison

He touches her, lightly.

They are playful at first, expressions high-pitched,
like sopranos, in full voice.

She rebuffs his advances, then poses, teasing,
like a coy lover, all bravado.

He touches her, lightly.

He's dressed to impress, two shades, each side of grey,
like a zebra, eye-catching.

He flashes fancy footwork, a dance of romance,
like Fred Astaire, with flair.

He touches her, lightly.

Two suitors watch on, biding their time,
like outsiders, envious.

Disturbed by voices, the four shadows flee,
like fugitives, hurriedly.

Finally, they settle, on pastures that invite,
like playmates, puffed out.

With a bit of a touch here
and some flapping there
– magpies, just having fun.

Real World

Flashback: Gonubie, South Africa

Looking down the river,
a murmur past dusk,
homes nestle in hills,
mist rises above *krantz*,
lights shimmer on mountainside,
boats with green lights
glide along giddily,
evade low-tide silt.

All is still,
except
for the
incessant
shiss shiss shiss
of Christmas
beetles.

Tonight,
the moon does not shed its glow,
bush and tree shadows
are cast by pavement lights.

From the quiet
a TV blares:
Bomb blast,
two dead,
80 injured.

Reality breaks
the spell.

Desire

Our bond strengthens
as she dwells upon her drink.

Day after day, we wake from rest,
welcome the new dawn
with its promise of affection.

Each morning, she glances my way, shyly;
I ponder with delight the
soundless moments we'll share.

Each night, she's a constant companion;
I unwind in her presence
as she dwells upon her drink.

In time, I detect change.

Her complexion fades.
   She stoops.
 Shrivels.
      Her perfume,
once a playful tickle at my nostrils,
    no longer yields its bouquet.
Though she dwells still upon her drink,
  she's no longer what she was.

There's no option: I dump her.

Weeks later, I yearn for her still
– that single yellow rose
in a glass full of water.

Fragments

Who walked this track before me?

Who left, due west,
this ancient abode built rock by rock,
now a desolate ruin,
crumbling stone by stone?

Who walked this track before me?

Who left, due east,
this stormwater drain, built pipe by pipe,
now a harvester of waste,
growing tufts of fodder?

Who walked this track before me?

Who left, due south,
this pile of rejected chattels, built into an ant mound,
now an eyesore,
rusting week by week?

Who walked this track before me?

Who left, due north,
this oasis of wetlands, built by caring hands,
now a nature refuge,
flourishing from nothing?

Who walked these tracks before me?

Homeless

I'm on the run in the air 'cos I lost me home,
screeches Mr Corella.
Me too,
says his mate, and her mate,
and other shrieking mates.

I'm on the run in the air 'cos I need a new house,
screeches Mr Corella.
Me too,
says his mate, and her mate,
and more shrieking mates.

I'm on the run in the air 'cos there's no place to park,
screeches Mr Corella.
Me too,
says his mate, and her mate,
and many shrieking mates.

I'm on the run in the air 'cos there's no more trees,
screeches Mr Corella.
Me too,
says his mate, and her mate,
and scores of shrieking mates.

I'll be on the run in the air till I find a new joint,
screeches Mr Corella.
So – suck up our shrieks,
you whinging humans,
'cos,
unlike me and me mates,
you haven't lost your home.

On the Farm

Flashback: Oudtshoorn, South Africa

Clip-clip, clip-clip.
The woman's straw hat is visible from afar.
It shelters her face.
The woman bends, rises, stretches, bends again.
Clip-clip, clip-clip.
Her snippers invade the silence.

Amid shadows of giant gums and unkempt bush,
the sun's rays peep their hellos.
The woman in the straw hat stoops within the gaps.
Clip-clip, clip-clip.

A dog drifts in from nowhere, sidles up to greet her.
The woman stretches, bends; strokes the uninvited guest.

The woman resumes her task: clears, cuts, trims, snips.
Clip-clip, clip-clip.

She strives to clear choked nature, to allow it to breathe,
to taste freedom, to again reach for the sky.

In return, nature sighs its gratitude.
Cool gusts wave at the woman,
caress her as she stoops, rises, stretches, bends
amid echoes of
clip-clip, clip-clip.

Thank you, the air whispers. *Thank you.*

The woman in the straw hat bends into the breeze;
renews her crusade to return the light.
Clip-clip, clip-clip.

Wonder Drug

Heavy with worry,
she recollects the
sedative's ancient use,
both cosmetic and medicinal.

Listless, she ponders its potency…
will it still her for sleep?

Abruptly,
    she
slashes
         at its base,
    as if
ripping
         an infant from a breast.

Later,
    she sniffs its
         scent,
drifting
   from beneath her pillow.

Finally subdued,
once more she inhales
the fragrance of
the snip of
lavender.

Two Roses

Sombre mist
shrouds
unkempt cemetery.

Five years on,
she recalls
past times,
sheds tears for
her mum and dad,
here,
so near,
so untouchable.

She pauses,
head bowed
as a blossom
sags at dusk.

Eyes closed, she
searches to embrace
faded memories.

On each grave she lays
a matching rose,
fleeting symbols of
two lives

cut

short.

Now What?

They hurry, scurry.
Like armies
on parade, they
march to a frantic beat.

All know their roles for
as long as they live in
their regimented world.

Busy, busy, they bustle,
day in, day out.
There's no time for rest.
Alert to tasty tidbits,
morsels large or lumpy,
workers slog for their lot.

Smart, they sense danger.
At any hint of rain,
bums up, little legs
t wi t ch
like cyclists on speed.
They know
what has to be done
before the heavens open up.

But, on a clear day,
what do these ants think
when a sprinkler is turned on?

Contrast

Listen:
Sounds Of
Men Chin-wagging
Axes Chopping
Timber Splitting
Chainsaws Roaring
Trees Crashing.
Noise!

listen…

sounds of

cows ruminating

butterflies nestling

feathers floating

leaves curling

one claw clapping…

silence.

Living the Dream

Early start to the day, feathered crew are away
searching for fresh bounty, including tasty cray.

With no bite in sight, there is little to do
except stay alert in the hope of a chew.

Spotting returned fishermen from far away,
starving, they all swoop on the catch of the day.

A regal landing, despite feeling weary,
Pick me, pick me, one pelican yells clearly.

Jostling at first for spots among friends turned foes,
pink bill to the fore, she then goes with the flow.

Whole fish, bones or innards – it's all heaven-sent;
once she swallows her fill, she floats; she's well spent.

Short nap later; watching the large bird in flight
you'll agree there is nothing wrong with her diet.

A wing-span stretching wide, her effortless glide
makes a splendid sight as she looks down with pride.

At dusk, as day whispers its farewell, so does she,
beneath a washed-up ship on the edge of the sea.

Mother Worries

What will our future hold?
The young mum ponders,
gazing at infinity,
while her brood,
carefree,
plays on a sunny day.

She marvels at the hills
that watch over her
in their expansiveness.

She relishes the open spaces
that allow her to tread
on their vastness.

She delights at the wetlands
that welcome her to wade
within their depths.

She frets at the urban sprawl
that encroaches on her domain
with creeping tentacles.

What will our future hold?
The young mum ponders,
gazing at infinity,
while her brood,
carefree,
plays on a sunny day
         – and she clings tightly to her joey.

Who's the Boss Then?

At home,
paws up against door,
he balances on hind legs
then…back on all fours
nudges the glass pane,
implores attention.
Nut-brown eyes scream, *Walk me – or you're not my mate.*

In bushland,
he takes the lead,
stops here, sniffs there,
does his business, hind legs
shovel dirt to hide the deed.
Poo-bag in hand, I stoop to collect.
Nut-brown eyes yell, *Good job – and don't forget to bin it.*

On the shore,
he's eager for action,
pounds soft dunes,
attacks wild waves,
then shakes himself dry
and worships the sun.
Nut-brown eyes shout, *Enough – my tummy needs filling.*

Back home,
he's primed to devour;
chicken necks, a scoop of gravy,
aromas drive him on a crazy dance.
Bowl is placed; within seconds
licked clean as a dishwashed plate.
Nut-brown eyes suggest, *Not bad – any chance of more*?

In the lounge,
snug in woollen coat, he
curls by fireplace flames.
A damp nose jabs my hand.
I succumb to the hint,
knead the bundle of muscle.
Nut-brown eyes smile, *Thanks, mate – time to tuck me in.*

Always There

She cherishes it,
clasps it close to her chest.

Amid wild seas,
froth filters through fingers as waves yearn for rest,
din of crash upon crash upon crash bends ears,
gulls dip for fresh fish within crests of swell surge,
stink of salt-saturated seaweed invades nostrils,
shades of blue, grey and ruby blur late-day landscape.

Amid dense bush,
trees big and small stretch limbs every which way,
winged warblers chatter wildly as they vie for a perch,
silhouettes dart warily as their joeys jig for a feed,
scent of eucalypt rises and falls in still air,
shadows shift, usurp sunlight to mark fall of the day.

Nature –
always there to hug her with gusto,
like a forever friend.

Pointless

A thing of beauty (no longer) is a joy forever – John Keats

Willows weep on the fringes,
silent, still,
at onset of dusk.

Under cover of darkness,
wielding weapons to shatter,
vandals
        strike.

       Frenzied,
  they mutilate:
    c . h - o , p
  c - u \ t
     h ' a) c ~ k
   s / l / a \ s /h.

Fragile saplings drop:
lopped,
carved,
sliced,
severed.

Silent, at break of dawn,
on the fringes,
willows weep, still.

Ostrich Palace

Flashback: Oudtshoorn, South Africa

Like a lover, the veldt draws you in,
sucks at your psyche so it cannot be scorned.

Ensconced within a membrane
of mountain mist
lies a dust bowl,
a desert, deserted mostly,
except for *Welgeluk*,
the ostrich palace,
ornate yet not ostentatious,
a portrait of stately significance,
built at the peak of the feather boom.

It stands statuesque,
a monument to an era of consequence.
An oasis of lush green and wrap-around veranda
entices friends and strangers into its folds,
welcomes them with sighs that linger.

As the palace captures your heart,
mountains and veldt look on,
motionless,
embracing all securely in its grasp.

Missing You

Oh, sweet thing, I will weep for you,
I will miss you all when you're gone.

I love that you're a constant companion,
your glow brightens life when the chill shivers in.
I love that you snuggle into stray spots,
you wink your greetings – and alter my landscape.

Oh, sweet thing, I will sob for you,
I will miss you all when you're gone.

I love that you shelter those around you,
your shudders I feel as you brave bitter breezes.
I love that you selflessly share your space,
you're never alone, you and your many mates.

Oh, sweet thing, I will cry for you,
I will miss you all when you're gone.

I love that you don't give a damn for your haters,
you're my beacon through winter's gloom.
I love that when spring squints from slumber,
your gleaming yield will still stir fond memories.

Oh, sweet thing, I will weep for you,
I will miss you all when you're gone.

Yes, you – and the trillion, trillion, trillion other
sour sobs.

Nightlife

Haiku 1

Silvery ripples
move to and fro like fireflies.
Bright moon contemplates.

Part 2

Shades of Bleak

> Only in the darkness
> can you see the stars.
>
> Martin Luther King Jr

Why Him?

Flashback: Angolan Border

I

Just a boy,
he went to fight a war,
a war for men.

Barely adult,
he'd scarcely savoured
silliness of adolescence.

Instead,
pimple-faced,
he braved
obstacles,
challenges,
fears
no man should confront.

He knew little of
parade grounds,
machine guns,
strange landscapes.
He knew nothing of his enemies,
only that his country said they were.
He fought
shadows,
silent silhouettes.

Nine months later,
still 18,
the boy came back.

In a body bag.

II

I had to identify the corpse.

His ID tag lay
listless,
as a noose.

I felt sadness.
Especially, I felt guilt:
I wasn't there to watch his back.

Because that time,
on that day,
the day a bullet
sealed his destiny,
it was my fate to be the pen pusher.

It was not my time.

Forty years on,
only guilt
survives.

Tangled Web

Love and hate –
woven
within
the family
web.

Precious children:
often
kind,
loyal,
adored;
sometimes
        frustrating,
  infuriating,
        mind-warping.

Is there excuse for abuse?
Can children
drive parents that far?

When the mind
SNAPS,
the
web
di s in te gr a te s.

Senseless

for my nephew

Death called
too soon
for a child
yet to blossom.

Think on the young
whose shoots are
crushed
before fruition.

Then ponder upon
Nicky, just a bud
amidst the bunch:
inquisitive,
talkative,
a flower-child
who will never
bloom.

Dear God, why

pick

the innocents?

A Mother's Grief

for Anne-Marie Mykyta

Why? Why was her daughter murdered?

For most, day wakes.
        For her, night persists.

For most, breakfast chats.
        For her, a vacant seat.

For most, school's in.
        For her, an empty desk.

For most, spring blooms.
        For her, eternal winter.

For most, family joy.
        For her, a missing child.

For most, sun shines.
        For her, darkness of hell.

For most, friends' laughter.
        For her, deathly silence.

For most, beach scents.
        For her, seaweed stench.

For most, evening meals.
        For her, tasteless tidbits.

For most, the night sleeps.
        For her, more nightmares.

Why? Why was her daughter murdered?

On the Precipice

Distraught, she
    sits near
  wetlands' edge.
Wild eyes
    search nature
for strength.
She glances down,
      tears at
    unkempt hair.
She stumbles
    towards
    beckoning depths.

She stops,
turns,
  looks
at her daughters:
    twins, two-year-olds.
They look back at her.

She steps towards them.
      Her hands
    convulse on the pram.

A violent pause.

      She
  releases
    the
  brake…

G'day Ann, you out walking the girls then?
Startled, she turns to face the voice.
In silence, she steps towards her neighbour,
hugs her for saving more than she will ever know.

Merrilyn

Flashback: Port Elizabeth, South Africa

Were you a slave?
Or a servant?

You arrived early.
You left late.
Every weekday.

You
cleaned our house,
made our beds,
washed our dishes,
cooked our meals.
Every weekday.

Even after five years, we never knew you,
only that you had children (how many?),
and you lived in a nearby township
from where you walked to and from work
in sunshine, wind or rain.
Every weekday.

After tending our needs at trifling cost,
you must have gone back to your shack,
to your children, and you would've had to
clean your house,
make your beds,
wash your dishes,
cook your meals.
Every weekday.

Were you a servant?
Or a slave?

The Parting

Sunday. Twilight. Damp.
Trio sinks into train seats,
Sister, brother flank big, bearded dad.
He smiles, hauls out new gadget.
His children giggle back,
mesmerised by the device…and him.

I love you, Daddy.
I love you too, Daddy.

They play with no care,
content as any family; bonded.

End of line looms, like a cloudburst.
He smiles again, embraces each child.
Showers of tears fall.
His children cling to him. He to them.

I love you, Daddy.
I love you too, Daddy.

They disembark into chill,
climb steps to their other lives.
Their hands clutch as if there is no tomorrow.

In bleakness, the siblings' mum awaits;
gnaws at her nails.
Sadness spits as the big, bearded man bear-hugs her.
They unhinge.
She turns to her children.

I love you, Mummy.
I love you too, Mummy.

The train shunts forward like life before the crash.

Changing World 1

Song of Innocence & Experience

She falls.
She cries.
Her teacher looks on.
She cries still.
She wants to be consoled.
A hug will do.

Her teacher hovers…

                        …walks away.

He knows better than to touch the child.

Changing World 2

Song of Innocence & Experience

In a park one day,
as his grandfather
and great-grandfather
did before him,
a man
sits his
granddaughter
on his lap.

Then he remembers:
this is something he ought not do.

Through My Eyes

for Dorothy, my mother-in-law

I'm not what you see.
I'm not this piss-weak, grimacing individual.
I'm not this wheelchair-bound vegetable.
I'm not helpless, hopeless, nothing.

I'm alive.
I have a brain. It works. Perfectly.

I just can't make you understand me
because my words are no longer words.
They are gurgles, babbles – and sobs of rage.
I desperately want you to understand what I say.

But no one does,
except my daughter.
Hour after hour, day after day,
her lap cradles the alphabet board.
I nod as she guesses one of 26 letters.
It seems to take a lifetime to guess each letter.
That's what it takes to understand me.
So no one does,
except my daughter.

Finally,
I'm too tired.
It's too painful to nod.
My daughter's patience is endless.
Mine has run out.

I've become what you see:
a piss-weak, grimacing individual,
a wheelchair-bound vegetable…
helpless,
hopeless,
nothing.

My brain works perfectly, but…
I'm no longer alive.

Please understand.

Caged Within

Circled signs reveal a speed limit
       – but the race is on.

In and out, in and out
flicker, flicker, flicker
fast, faster, fastest
all shades, shapes, sizes
boxed within four lines, two broken,
hell-bent on reaching who knows where.

Circled signs reveal a new limit
       – but the race persists.

In and out, in and out
flicker, flicker, flicker
fast, faster, fastest
all shades, shapes, sizes
boxed within two lines, one broken,
hell-bent on reaching who knows where.

Spectator bridges, soaring lamp posts,
swaying flora, screaming graffiti
wave to
these highway hoons
trapped within
       – four lines
       – two lines
       – their cars
       – themselves
       – their souls
until the red-green lights signal
the race has ended and they are free to go
       – to who knows where.

Mind-field

Life –
so
challenging,
wearying,
exhausting…

so
un finish ed.

Death –
no
challenges,
weariness,
exhaustion…

so
finished.

Is there
any point
toiling for
more
        more
more
                more
        more
more
        and more
any more?

Or is there light at the end of all tunnels?

Lucky Us

Count your blessings
if you can hear, see or walk.
Consider yourself lucky your life is here.

Count your blessings
if you can hear,
thanks to an ear device or a wax clean-out.
Consider others deafened by bomb blasts.

Count your blessings
if you can see,
thanks to spectacles or a magnifying glass.
Consider others blinded by shrapnel.

Count your blessings
if you can walk,
thanks to a hip operation or aid of a frame.
Consider others with limbs severed in wars.

Count your blessings
if you can hear, see or walk.
Consider yourself lucky you're still alive.

Street Cents

Christmas is coming, and the grub is lined up.
Please put two dollars in a hungry soul's cup
If you haven't got two dollars, a dollar will do;
if you haven't got a dollar, then join the queue.

Dis **o** r d e r

It's never 'Happy birthday'.
        To her, it's always 'Dappy hirthbay'.
She's just dumb, sniggers a mate.
        She's just an idiot, sniggers another.

She's in a world of pain
        – but no one listens.

It's never 'Pot of gold'.
        To her, it's always 'Bot of dolg'.
She's still dumb, sniggers a mate.
        She's still an idiot, sniggers another.

She's in a world of pain
        – but no one listens.

It's never 'Goodbye, mates'.
        To her, it's always 'Moodbye, gates'.
She'll always be dumb, sniggers a mate.
        She'll always be an idiot, sniggers another.

She's in a world of pain
        – but no one listens.

And
        when
they
              finally
        find
her,
        itistoo   late.

Alfred

Flashback: Port Elizabeth, South Africa

As usual, you arrive drunk.

You come to
mow lawns,
trim garden edges,
prune blooms, bushes.

You lunch on
thick brown bread slices,
thinly buttered,
heaped with baked beans,
slopped into your tin plate,
washed down with
strong, black coffee
in your tin mug.

As usual, you leave sober.

Cash in hand,
you hit the *shebeens*
to end the night as
you began the day.

I reflect on your life. And mine.

If I had been born black
in an era of apartness,
would I have been
a drunk – or
a freedom fighter?

Apart

Woken by bitter wind and driving rain,
he shudders into the splintered bench.
He fidgets and shivers, as if fevered.
He buries deeper into the worn coat.

Soon, in St Vinnies' hand-me-downs,
he stakes his spot on trampled tiles.
His sign begs for a few dollars to help
shroud him from another endless day.

He mourns for his family: his wife and
grown-up sons, no longer a part of him.
He grieves for his spirited daughter,
now a corpse rotting underground.

He checks the tattered cap, notes its
emptiness mirrors his state of mind.
He dozes fitfully, sounds of the few coins
fail to rouse him from his muffled reality.

Later, as sunset casts sombre shadows, he
caresses the cursed bottle, unscrews its top.
Soon, the pain will wane, at least until
tomorrow…should a new day dawn for him.

Lottery

Go through proper channels?
Or take a boat?
Rely on authorities?
Or believe smugglers?

He weighs up the gamble.

Cash changes hands.
Blackness falls.
With faceless others,
his family boards.

Their eyes spell trust.

Out at sea, hemmed in by water;
not the kind to quench thirsts.
Miserly morsels feed heaving guts.
Ruthless sun scorches its victims.

Relentless, days follow days.
Cries of the trusting haunt him:
I want to go home, Daddy!
When will we get there, Daddy?

One more bleak dawn emerges,
one more cycle to break hearts.

Shore is sighted.
Race against time.
Leaking boat.
Giant waves.

Will they live?
Or will they lose
this lottery of life?

Lost Chance

He arrives with an
invisible suitcase
filled with dreams…

…a boat person,
trip from hell
via Vietnam;
devoted dad
works to live
lives to work
hits lofty peak
– SA's State Governor.

Years later…

…a boat person,
trip from hell
via Afghanistan;
devoted dad
will work to live
will live to work
can hit lofty peak
– even SA's State Governor.

No.

There will be no more boat people
– only invisible bodies
with suitcases
full of nightmares.

Stranger in Silk

Upright,
as a needle jabbed into yarn, he stands.

Dressed
in tatty shirt,
        left behind by some bloke when it got
        in the way of a tangle with his chick;
in ragged jumper,
        dumped in a wheelie bin by a wife
        weary of her hubby in mended garb;
in faded pants,
        op-shop bought judging by its length,
        a darn short of covering scarred ankles;
in shabby shoes,
        someone's favourite pair, no longer
        able to be patched by any Mr Fixit;
in intricate headdress,
        a criss-cross of crimson flashed in faces
        of those not sure what to make of him.

His turban defines him.

For now, he bides his time,
collects trolleys from car park
hour by hour, day by day, week by week, month by month.

I pass him by on most shop visits.
He's upright still,
like a needle poked into yarn, he stands.

What stories has he to share?

Stepping Stones

Like a toddler, he tries to walk,
takes baby steps, until he
folds and falls.

He rights himself,
takes more small steps,
tumbles again.

Roused by those who know,
he trudges once more
into an unstable future.

Up he gets, off he goes. Wobbles.
Feels secure. Until again, he
folds and falls.

Battered,
like a boxer pummelled, he
picks himself off the canvas.

Like a toddler, he pushes on,
one more baby step at a time,
one more tiny step in front of the next.

At last, his
steps grow to
strides, become steady.

He knows the slog
to stand tall, to not fold, to not fall,
will be hard. Always.

Such a crippling bastard is
Grief.

Eerie

Haiku 2

Shades of blood at dusk.
Trees cast shadows in foreground.
Darkness envelops.

Part 3

Let in the Light

Do not take life too seriously.
You will never get out of it alive.

Elbert Hubbard

Attitude

So, listen up, kid…

Just 'cos me hair's gone grey
don't mean I'm Father Christmas,
so don't gawk like I'm ancient
        – 'cos I'm not.

Just 'cos I got lines down me face
don't mean I'm a road map,
so don't smirk like I'm an alien
        – 'cos I'm not.

Just 'cos I gotta walkin' frame
don't mean I can't budge me butt,
so don't scowl like I'm in the way
        – 'cos I'm not.

Just 'cos I packed on me winta gear
don't mean I'm a fat bastard,
so don't reckon I'm a binge-eater
        – 'cos I'm not.

Just 'cos I got varicose veins
don't mean I'm on me last legs,
so don't gape like I'm gonna cark it
        – 'cos I'm not.

So, listen up, kid…

Just 'cos yer
younger
handsomer
quicker
thinner
fitter
don't mean yer any *happier* than me,
so bloody well don't think yer are
       – 'cos you're not.

Horror Show

Lights. Sunnies. Action.

No, not a movie set.
Instead, the scenario
awakens
a childhood nightmare:
I'm home alone,
panicked victim
of night-shift parents.
Doors deadlocked,
windows barred,
a prison within house's shelter.
I'm stuck like a rabbit snared.
My screams
shriek
down desolate
streets,
bounce back
like echoes lost.
No help. No escape. Trapped.

Lights. Sunnies. Action.

Again, I recall the scenario,
remember especially:
No help. No escape. Trapped.

This time though,
I'm sitting in a dentist's chair.

Dad's Delight

First child,
a boy,
squishy as a
reeled-in squid.

New daddy flashbacks:
sloppy
 smooches
  smother
   shell-shape ears,
    chubby cheeks,
   crinkly eyes,
  clogged nostrils,
killer smiles;
non-stop legs
         k a r a t e - k i c k
heaven
in
random delight;
wee toes
         w r i g g l e
amid
clouds of Johnson's baby powder.

First child,
now a man,
solid as a
nugget of gold.

Can't Live Without You

Irresistible,
long and slender,
no sign of padding,
firm to the touch,
yet smooth as
sanded wood.

I get to a point where
I can no longer ignore
the sleek outline,
slight ridges
perfectly formed.

From its resting place,
I lift
the object of my fancy,
fondle
its form
between
thumb and forefinger.

I indulge.

Lightly,
then firmly,
finally,
I put to paper
my precious
HB pencil.

Face of Change

Mirror, mirror on the wall,
who's the fairest of them all?
Used to be you, it replied.
But you're haggard now, you see,
not at all like you used to be.

OK mirror, mirror on the wall,
how can I once again stand tall?
Fast walking will help, it replied.
Tummy tuck if you've got the cash,
false teeth if you want to look flash.

Mirror, mirror on the wall,
appears I need an overhaul.
Got more tips for you, it replied.
Lay off ciggies, fatty grub and booze,
and cut out that mid-arvo snooze.

Mirror, mirror on the wall,
sorry I asked who's fairest of all.
You've shamed me, made me squirm.
Yet I'm content with the way I am,
'cos at my age, I don't give a damn.

All Together Now

Flashback: Cape Town, South Africa

The music is alive.

By the sea,
on a stage as big
as a giant drafts board,
they jive to the tug of jazz;
a kaleidoscope of
races rocking to the
samba of togetherness.

The music pauses.

They swap partners,
wait, touch again as
rhythms up a beat,
then
bodies shake,
thighs clash,
smiles shower an admiring throng.

The music dies.

Dancers
bow to consorts,
peck their farewells,
wave their goodbyes;
know tomorrow
will throb to a different pulse.

Gimme Five

Where would we be without our two-by-fives?

They
fondle ear lobes,
invade nostrils,
don make-up,
twirl curls,
adjust bra straps,
wriggle jocks,
scratch bums.

How would we do without our two-by-fives?

They
clutch wallets,
direct choirs,
tie balloons,
skim piano keys,
flick phone photos,
type texts,
rip open Chrissie gifts.

What would we do without our
two
lots
of
five
flexible
fingers?

Ship Shapes

First cruise

They scoffed it all, bar the fruit & veg.

After breakfast,
her thighs spreadeagled a heaving chair
like squished pumpkin halves,
his belly sagged sadly over long shorts
like a pregnant paw-paw.

They scoffed it all, bar the fruit & veg.

After lunch,
her boobs jiggled in too-tiny bikini
like pips peeking from pomegranates,
his speedos stretched to clasp its bounty
like spuds bursting from their sacks.

They scoffed it all, bar the fruit & veg.

After dinner,
she squeezed into sequinned dress
like a cauliflower stuffs its stalk,
he crammed into bloated tuxedo
like a melon fills its wrapping.

They scoffed the bloody lot;
all they left us was the fruit & veg.

Grandpa's Lament

It is not as smashing as you might think.
Retirement larks haven't tickled me pink.

For starters, this new downsizing idea
means less room for us both – and that is clear.

Drives me batty when she gets in the way.
And when I scowl, not amused she will say:

*The shed will be perfect, it's crystal clear,
for all your trash, so stack it in there, dear.*

When I come inside and use the remote,
Don't flick, flick, flick is her usual quote.

One morning we discuss using the car:
It's darts day, I say, *I can't walk that far.*

So we drive to the library to read…
then rush home 'cos the dog's needing a feed.

Once I liked a drop with mid-morning brunch.
Frowns now mean I have to wait until lunch.

Then she eats vegan at some highbrow place
and winces at my burger with distaste.

More family and friends visit lately;
I'm nagged to keep the house looking stately.

We are always babysitting the clan.
If I don't nappy change, poo hits the fan.

Nowadays she's buying fancy wooden signs
that imply I'm hopeless in silly rhymes.

No, retirement's not as great as you'd think.
Bugga me – thought it would tickle me pink!

New Breed

Muscles bulge,
tendons tighten,
ligaments lengthen.

Daily,
their
sandshoes
scrunch
gravel on
pathways
and pavements.

Their eyes fix on
routes ahead.
Visors shade the sun,
vests soak up sweat,
lycra hides thick thighs.

They sacrifice chit-chat,
don't stop for dawdlers.

They're frenzied, fanatic, obsessed.

They're
stress-busters,
carting cosseted cargo.

They're
new age
parents, pushing prams.

Carpe Diem

Family counsel

She is dubbed *The Procrastinator* by those who care.
Everyone calls her negative; unwilling to grab 'now'.
I am asked to change her life; that seems a tall order.
Zilch chance, they all say; she is afraid of the present.
Everyone's sure her pessimism & disorder will reign.

There're times when we bleed tears of rage and fury.
Hell and back we go, clutching at sparks of optimism.
Everyone (mates and foes) declares there is no hope.

Daybreak mumbles a fatigued *Hello!* in Week Eleven.
And it's on this day she decides to make the promise:
Yesterday was then – from now on, I will *seize the day*.

Young Mind

To do, or not to do?
That is the question.

He's a sports jock.
He covets success.
If he does it,
he'll have the edge,
advance his career.

Some of his mates do it.
Many women do it.
Once done,
all is
smooth,
sleek, and
soft to the stroke.

Again,
he ponders the question.

He opts to do.

Carefully,
awkwardly,
he leans the
blade
beside his skin – and
begins to shave his legs.

Seat Lotto

On the 3 p.m. train,
two seats across the way are empty
        – at first.
Soon, the window seat across the way
fills with a man
in carefully pressed pants;
in cream shirt, secured by black silk tie;
his mouth full of whitened teeth.
A banker, perhaps, judging by:
the briefcase clutched in manicured fingers,
the way he blows into his Kleenex,
the potent lavender deodorant.
He dozes.

On the same train,
one seat across the way stays empty
        – for a while.

Soon, the seat across the way
fills with a bloke
in red-checked shorts;
in singlet, behind which grey hairs peek;
his gob full of stained teeth.
A battler, for sure, judging by:
the toaster in his Cheap as Chips bag,
the way he sneezes into his hanky,
the scent of hard-yakka sweat.
Not ready to doze.

Good day for it, mate, battler, sliding closer, tells the banker.
Hmm, the banker, shut-eyed and with shift of a cheek, replies.
Their conversation dies.
So does my amusement,
though I am grateful that…

on this 3 p.m. train,
the seat next to me does not fill
        – for the rest of the ride.

Colour Coded

Imagine how
differently
we would
picture the
world
if…

the sky was beige
        and grass lilac;

the sea was yellow
        and sand green;

tree trunks were blue
        and leaves indigo;

koalas were lime
and roos orange;

apples were grey
        and bananas pink;

carrots were magenta
        and cucumbers purple;

Crows' colours were black, white, teal and silver
        and Port Power's red, navy and gold?

Odd One Out

Every Aussie bloke has a shed.
So they say.

It's a home out of home, a joint to:
escape the missus and kids,
pin up naked floozies,
listen to the footy,
check out greyhounds on the telly,
play darts with yer mates,
reek of grease and sweat.
So they say.

Yep, a bloke's place is in his shed.
The bigger, the better.
The more junk, the better.
Sheds give you
space
to forget the squabbles,
time
to mull on things, by yerself.

Yep, every Aussie bloke must have a shed.
So they say.

Strewth, I reckon I'm missing out:
a small room in my house is my shed;
pencils, pens, PC and printer my playthings.

Glassy-eyed

They hit their target,
blur my vision.

Many lay motionless,
refuse to budge.
Others power
their way to
self-destruction below.

Later,
the immovable ones,
glistening as the
sun peeps through,
continue to
evade their
plunging lookalikes.

Insignificant
they seem, but
steadfast,
stable,
secure,
they mesmerise me.

In time,
they dry out,
yet blur my vision still
        – these droplets of rain upon my windowpane.

Spicy Scandal

Cooking course, hours long,
taste offerings the pull.
Sounds good, I tell my wife.
What can possibly go wrong?

It's a kitchen made in heaven:
lentils, turmeric, tur dal,
coriander, cumin and chilli –
Indian chefs' secret weapons.

More ingredients spice meat:
masala, onion, garlic, ginger;
together we cook, bake, fry –
Orient on a plate is such a treat.

We tempt friends for a sample.
I'm cooking my special, I say,
*you'll love the tangy flavours
and I'll make sure there's ample.*

With hours to spare, all is done;
aromas waft in nooks and crannies.
We welcome the doting couple,
she ripely pregnant with a son.

We observe, smell and swallow
as I conquer them with curry –
hot, hotter, hottest.
Stuffed, I relish cries of *Bravo*!

Later I text to check her fate.
Not too good, he stammers.
Rushed to hospital overnight.
He sighs, regretful of her state.

She went into sudden labour
soon after they got home.
Sadly, they never call again
to test my extra spicy flavour.

Last Strand

Silent.
Still.
Guised
as a
question
mark,
it arches
into the
wrinkled
sheet.

Gossamer thin.
Volcanic red.
Embedded.
Solitary.

It is all she's left behind.
In his palm, he
caresses it,
presses it to his cheek
        – this single strand of her hair, always his.

Travel Tribulations

The destination we love,
though slog to get there we don't
– and we're going to miss the dog.

In advance, we
update passports,
secure insurance,
book in extra luggage
– and decide who'll care for the dog.

Days before, we
secure windows,
lock sheds,
mow lawns
– and wash the dog spotless for his carer.

At the airport, we
avoid coughing passengers,
cringe at unruly kids,
observe travellers scurrying
– and worry that the dog will pine for us.

On the plane, we
fan away germs from the ill,
tire of toilet queues,
dodge recliner headrests
– and eat grub even the dog would avoid.

Destination (yes, lovely) is reached
– and though we face a slog to get back,
we know whose tail will wag when we're home.

Too Close for Comfort

We come together,
all with the same goal,
strangers, wide-eyed and aroused,
on a jaunt of expectation.

At the entrance,
we're handed fresh linen, masks,
and a toothbrush – for much later.

The air is thick
with the closeness of sweating bodies,
squished like sardines in a silver dish.

Soon we disrobe, each
reaching our own
boundaries in states of undress.

An orgy of arms and legs
flails for space
within our intimate meeting place.

As the clock ticks, limbs
search shamelessly for best spots,
mouths hang open, heads flop.

In time, fatigue overtakes
this symphony of togetherness,
passion for the exploration ends.

Erotic it's not.
We've had our fill of the torture chamber,
all of us – the strangers
aboard the long-distance flight to Africa.

Fired Up

Summer sizzles like snags on a barbie.
A stripping of singlets.
Let's shower, she says.
Yes, let's, says he.
Cold cascade cools craving
        – so, they're not quite done.

They feed on a feast of flathead and figs.
A clink of cocktails.
To us, she says.
To us, says he.
Wine wobbles her slightly witless
        – so, they're not quite done.

They sink into a bed warm as a sauna.
A spell of smooches.
Let's have more fun, she says.
Yes, let's, says he.
Like scorched snags on a barbie
        – finally, well and truly done.

Remember When

Haiku 3

They were the Sixties:
Beatles, hippies, peace, Kombis.
Yeah, those were the days.

Part 4

Water Runs Deep

The sea, once it casts its spell, holds one in its net of wonder forever.

Jacques Yves Cousteau

Locomotion

they
 d a n c e
   to no
   tune,
to and
 fro,   fro and
   to,
 this way and
   that,   that way
 and this

from one
  spot
to the
next,
     at random they

jump,

form shapes
  that twinkle,
glitter

they dart,
   skip, skip and
      dart,
 f l i c k e r
  like
fairy   lights

those
>   sparks of
> sunlight
> on serene
>   sea ripples,
>   to no
> tune they
>   *d a n   c e*

Just a Shoe

Tiny, torn, tattered –
it washes ashore at Moonlight Bay,
alluring inlet of shell-free sands,
see-through seas, shapely dunes, serrated cliffs.
Secluded.

Deadly.

What happened that day at Moonlight Bay?
Perhaps a woman soaked up the sun
on a yacht, where big waves run.
Later, she disappears.
Did she fall? Or was she pushed?
No body found. Just a shoe.
Was it a shark, out of the blue?

What happened that day at Moonlight Bay?
Perhaps a woman soaked up the sun
on the beach, where small waves run.
Later, she wades in too deep.
Did she drown? Or was she grabbed?
No body found. Just a shoe.
Was it a shark, out of the blue?

What did happen that day at Moonlight Bay?
No one knows, so you decide…

Tread lightly though as you wonder why
a shoe appeared
– and there was no goodbye.

Casting a Spell

Flashback: South Africa

Garden Route, Cape Province:
227 kilometres of beauty beckons;
a stretch
from Storms River
to Mossel Bay,
on the edge of an ocean.

Notice
nature's necklace of
beaches, cliffs, rocky capes,
and flourish of forests beyond.

In summer,
amble forever beside surf that speaks,
taste sea's take on sodium.

In spring,
sniff scents of blossoms,
witness blues, crimsons, yellows.

In autumn and winter,
gaze at early-rising mists
that veil hidden hamlets.

Magical places, aptly named:
Wilderness
Outeniqua
Tsitsikama
Fairy Knowe.

Is this the enchanted land?

As One

Watch
   wave
upon
   wave
upon
   wave
upon
   wave.

Like claws,
they curl,
then
clash,
splash.
Always
curling,
clashing,
splashing.

Calls from the deep deafen.

See.
Hear.

Sand.
Surf.
Smashing.
Sand.
Surf.
Smashing.

SightAndSoundMerge
UnbrokenTogetherForever

Satisfaction

Twisted fingers clasped,
they limp towards freedom,
that expanse of turquoise,
that ocean of fleeting liberty.

Battered by breakers,
brittle bones buckle
but the two old timers hold firm;
buoyancy brings glints of glee.

Arms flap like those of newborns
as the withered shapes
backstroke into seventh heaven,
float like beach balls bob on swells.

Sip of salvation sampled,
knotty fingers embrace afresh;
they wobble back with walking sticks
       – into the laps of twin walking frames.

Watchful Eye

Moon, that globe of gold,
casts light upon restless seas.
Stars skip on heaven's highway.
Green lights glow on distant tuna pens
as workers fatten catches.

More lights twinkle…
Fishermen chasing their prey?
A lighthouse warning of perils?
A lone yachtswoman sailing around her vast world?

Brighter lights beckon beyond
as the city refuses to bid its residents goodnight.

Sights stir emotions,
noises overpower senses.
Waves smash the shore, calling, calling.
Sinister sounds moan as sea scoots in and out of caves.

In heaven's silence,
gold gives way to silver,
mirrors a sliver of apple,
casts its wide smile.

After the Drowning

Sea's lament

I am hushed today, not my lively self.
It's my way of saying sorry.
I've always been a comfort,
but last night I was
callous, so unlike me.

I am hushed today, my sparkle is missing.
It's a sign of my compassion.
I've always been a strength,
but last night I was
heartless, so unlike me.

I am hushed today, the to-and-fro is gone.
It's to show I commiserate.
I've always soothed souls,
but last night I was
merciless, so unlike me.

How could I?

How could I
have so
callously,
heartlessly,
mercilessly
washed away
the life of that young child
delighting in the charm of me?

Bonding

Can we go to the beach today, Daddy?
Me and you – and take our old dog, Sadie?
    Yes sure son, why don't we give it a go?
    We can take the frisbee and have a throw.
We there yet, Daddy? It's always so far,
and the air con never works in your car.
    Please have some patience son, we'll soon be there.
    Careful the squid-jig! Don't let the seat tear!
At last, Daddy, just a couple more stairs.
Sand is hot, but got my thongs so who cares?
    Don't forget, son, the full slip, slop, slap.
    And be especially sure to wear your cap.
Think I'll swim first Daddy, I'm boiling hot.
You hold the lilo, the caps…yep, the lot.

I'm so cold now Daddy, really freezing.
If I don't get out soon, I'll keep sneezing.
    How about a go in those rock pools, son?
    If we're lucky, we'll find something for Mum.
Had enough of water Daddy; now what?
Why don't we have hot chips, sauce and the lot?
    But we haven't been at the beach that long.
    Surely your hunger pains can't be that strong.

Daddy, why don't we build castles of sand?
We've got buckets…hey, let's watch the band!
Forget 'em, Daddy. Let's fish at the docks.
We've got the rods so let's head to the rocks.
Hey, Daddy, we forgot to play cricket.
I brought bat and ball; you can keep wicket…

Thank you, Daddy, I had a ball today.
We should do it again sometime soon, hey?
> No worries, son. We had a ball in the sun.
> Down the track, we can look at a rerun.

How was your day at the beach, Hon,
just you and your energetic son?
> *Good, love, but I'm pretty much done.*
> *Bloody hell – he kept me on the run!*

Kicking Back

In the river cruise slipstream, commentary murmurs
amid animated chatter; no one listens, no one cares.

> Stories describe folk who toiled for yonks,
> past heroes who built a city from scratch.

Commentary murmurs amid animated chatter;
no one listens, no one cares in the river cruise slipstream.

> Tales tell of the tireless making their mark,
> present heroes who advance a great state.

Amid animated chatter, no one listens, no one cares;
in the river cruise slipstream, commentary murmurs.

> Yarns report those on the cusp of fortune,
> future heroes who will be worth billions.

No one listens, no one cares. In the river cruise slipstream,
commentary murmurs amid animated chatter.

> We sip one more shiraz as heroes' lives blur;
> a flotilla of tourists on a journey into haziness.

In the river cruise slipstream, commentary murmurs
amid animated chatter. Who listens? Who cares?

Ice Breaker

Awkward,
like a couple of copulating crabs,
they amble on to bleached shore.
He, red as a sunburnt lobster,
she, pale as Omo-scrubbed sheet.

Unsure,
like girl meets boy on a blind date,
they step into water, igloo-cold.
He, manfully, in tight Speedos,
she, shrieking, in bitsy bikini.

Happy,
like teens who draw love hearts,
they lark amid tangs of salt.
He, ducking in and out of waves,
she, splashing at frolics of foam.

Confident,
like a honeymoon twosome,
they stride on to sweltering sand.
He, boldly, takes her by the hand,
she, smiling, fingers clasped around his.

Quiet

A villanelle

Sounds of a river lull me calm
even if days are rushed or hushed.
I like the peace of distant farms.

All around there's a kind of charm.
It shifts the mood away from loud.
Sounds of a river lull me calm.

I start most mornings with a psalm;
even insects join in the hum.
I like the peace of distant farms.

Gums frolic in breeze, as do palms.
Garden vegies whisper *Hello*.
Sounds of a river lull me calm.

Nothing near to scare or alarm,
no one in sight to annoy or rile.
I like the peace of distant farms.

Days here are a shot in the arm;
all my troubles are left behind.
Sounds of a river lull me calm.
I like the peace of distant farms.

Serenity

Off Sellicks Hill (Haiku 4)

Hills, sky and Buddha.
At sea, two men in a boat.
Solitude, silence.

www.ingramcontent.com/pod-product-compliance
Lightning Source LLC
Chambersburg PA
CBHW070939080526
44589CB00013B/1573